SIGURD M. RASCHER

WILHELM HANSEN / Copenhagen

DISTRIBUTED BY

ED. 2952

A few words for the second edition.

No less so than 33 years ago, when these exercises were published for the first time, do I today address myself to the intelligent player, that is to the musician, for whom finger exercises are only a means to an end. Therefore I deem barlines to be superfluous, as they only would clutter up the overall picture. The structural element stems from the groups, now longer, now shorter. Their size is easily recognizeable; in No. 1 for example, the diminished chord descends and ascends for 8 tones each: the group consists of 16 tones. In No. 3 it shrinks to 12, in No. 5 to 8 tones, etc. Change of direction and change of chord coincide in No. 11; here the group has only 8 tones, in No. 13 only six, and so forth. Accidentals are used sparingly. Only where they are really necessary did I put them, that is within a group, or for tone alterations, or at chord changes. It follows that accidentals are not valid from one group to another. Is this clear, are natural signs mostly unnecessary and therefore omitted. Only where doubts might creep in will you find them; for instance at the change of lines and at the second note in a group; in fast reading this might help. I have also repeated an accidental here and there to clarify a fingering.*

To grant the player the greatest freedom, all exercises appear here in eighth notes. But it would be unnecessarily dull to play them only like that. Therefore the intelligent Saxophone Student (to him I turn with these studies !) will suit himself and select all kinds of variants, the more the better. I give here just a few. The player will invent unending variations and combinations and thus pleasantly broaden his sense for rhythm and style. To be a musician is his goal, not an acrobat with fingers.

September 5, 1968   *Sigurd M. Rascher*

Fingerings	Fingersätze

Fingerings are given here and there; their omission in other places is intentional. Within one group it will often be practical to use the same fingering.	Mit Absicht sind Fingersätze nicht überall angegeben. Innerhalb einer Gruppe sind sie oft unverändert anzuwenden.
Often more than one notation is possible (see No. 33 etc.). Since there is a pro and con to each of these, I have used now the one, now the other. This might be called inconsistent; it is, however, done on purpose because we are not always favored with »consistency« in real music.	Oft sind verschiedene Schreibweisen möglich (Nr. 33 etc.). Jede hat ihre Vor- und Nachteile. Darum habe ich bald die eine, bald die andere angewendet. Dies tat ich da wir auch in wirklicher Musik nicht immer mit Folgerichtigkeit begünstigt werden.
Example of reasoning for a certain fingering:	Erklärung seines Fingersatzes:

Nr. 37

| *Db is the first tone in a new group, hence rhythmically prominent. Avoid therefore here change of register between groups, lest the Db becomes much too prominent.* | Des ist der erste Ton in der neuen Gruppe, darum rhythmisch prominent. Langenwechsel ist deshalb hier zu vermeiden, um nicht noch mehr Betonung auf Des zu legen. |

Side Key with second finger right.

Seiten Klappe mit dem rechten Zeigefinger.

Keep right second finger down.

Rechter Zeigefinger bleibt liegen.

Keep right middlefinger down.

Rechter Mittelfinger bleibt liegen.

Many saxophones retain independent action of the spatulae for the left fifth finger. Here it is practical to depress those for Ab and C♯ simultaneously.

Viele Saxophone bieten unabhängige Bewegungsmöglichkeit der Tasten für den linken 5. Finger. Hier ist es praktisch die As und Cis Tasten gleichzeitig nieder zu drücken.

Open C♯

Offenes Cis

like low C♯ with octave Key.

wie das tiefe Cis, jedoch mit Oktav Klappe.

Not all Saxophones offer this possibility.

Nicht alle Saxophone bieten diese Möglichkeit.

Common fingering with right 5th finger.

Gewöhnlicher Fingersatz mit dem rechten 5. Finger.

Intentional! Learn to use your left 2nd finger!

Absichtlich! Lerne den linken Zeigefinger zu gebrauchen!

Examples of optional fingerings:

Verschiedene Möglichkeiten:

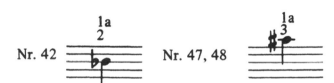

Nr. 42   Nr. 47, 48

Nr. 103

Similar choices are often possible - all should be tried.

Es ist gut verschiedene Fingersätze zu üben.

Nr. 44

Nr. 45

A few rhythms

Einige Rhytmen

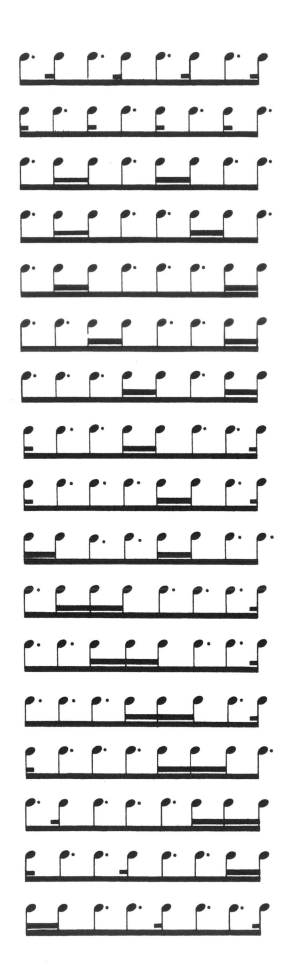

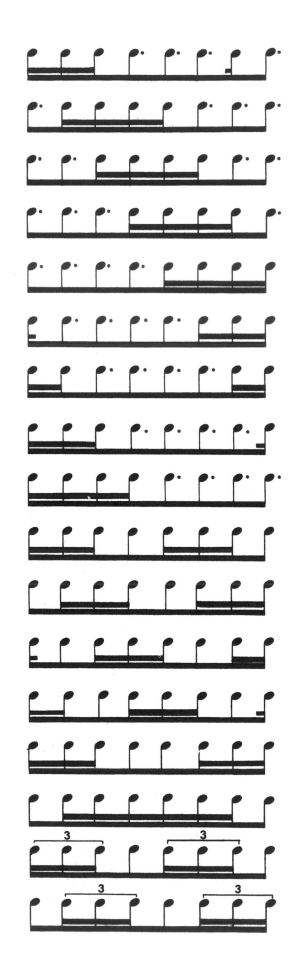

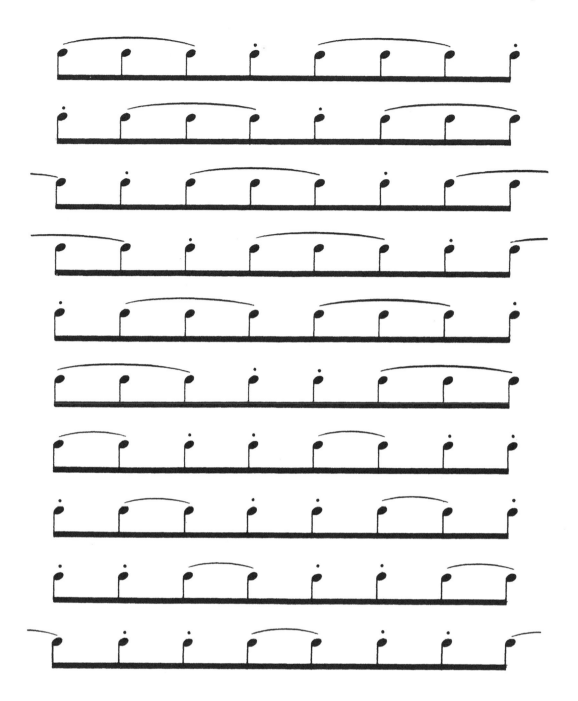

I

The Exercises may also be played in the following order:
Die Übungen können auch in folgender Reihenfolge gespielt werden:

1 - 27 - 49 - 59 - 69 - 79 - 89 - 99 - 109 - 119

2 - 28 - 50 - 60 - 70 - 80 - 90 - 100 - 110 - 120

5 - 29 - 51 - 61 - 71 - 81 - 91 - 101 - 111 - 121

6 - 30 - 52 - 62 - 72 - 82 - 92 - 102 - 112 - 122

7 - 31   17 - 39

8 - 32   18 - 40

9 - 33   23 - 45

10 - 34   24 - 46

11 - 35 - 53 - 63 - 73 - 83 - 93 - 103 - 113 - 123

12 - 36 - 54 - 64 - 74 - 84 - 94 - 104 - 114 - 124

15 - 37 - 55 - 65 - 75 - 85 - 95 - 105 - 115 - 125

16 - 38 - 56 - 66 - 76 - 86 - 96 - 106 - 116 - 126

19 - 41 - 129 - 133 - 137 - 141 - 145

20 - 42 - 130 - 134 - 138 - 142 - 146

25 - 47 - 131 - 135 - 139 - 143 - 147

26 - 48 - 132 - 136 - 140 - 144 - 148

21 - 43 - 57 - 67 - 77 - 87 - 97 - 107 - 117 - 127

22 - 44 - 58 - 68 - 78 - 88 - 98 - 108 - 118 - 128

158 SAXOPHONE EXERCISES

Sigurd M. Rascher

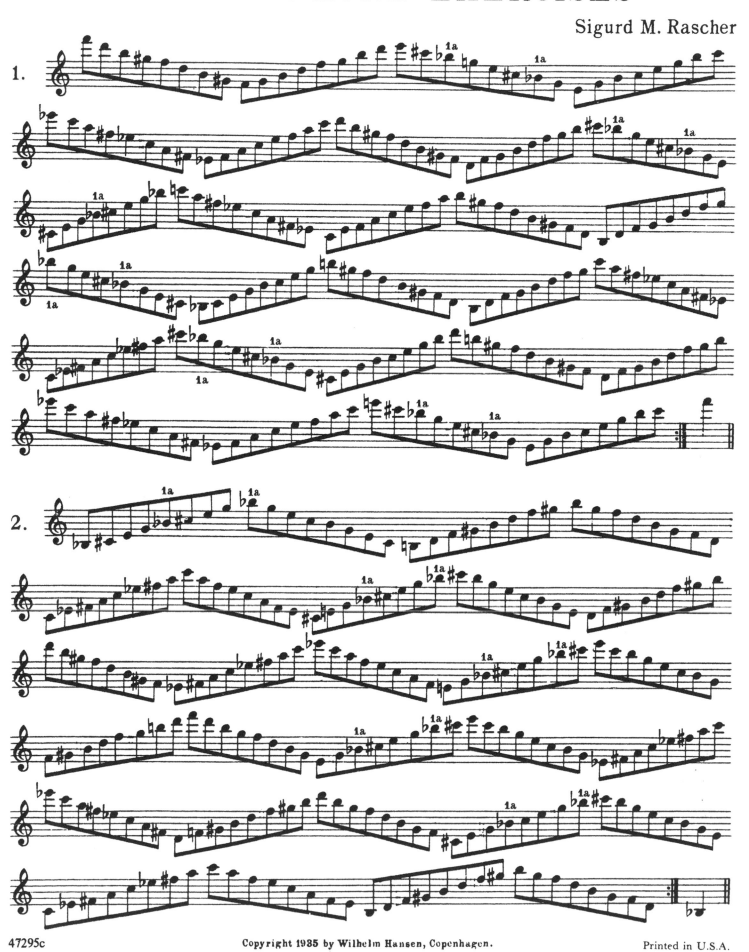

47295c

Printed in U.S.A.

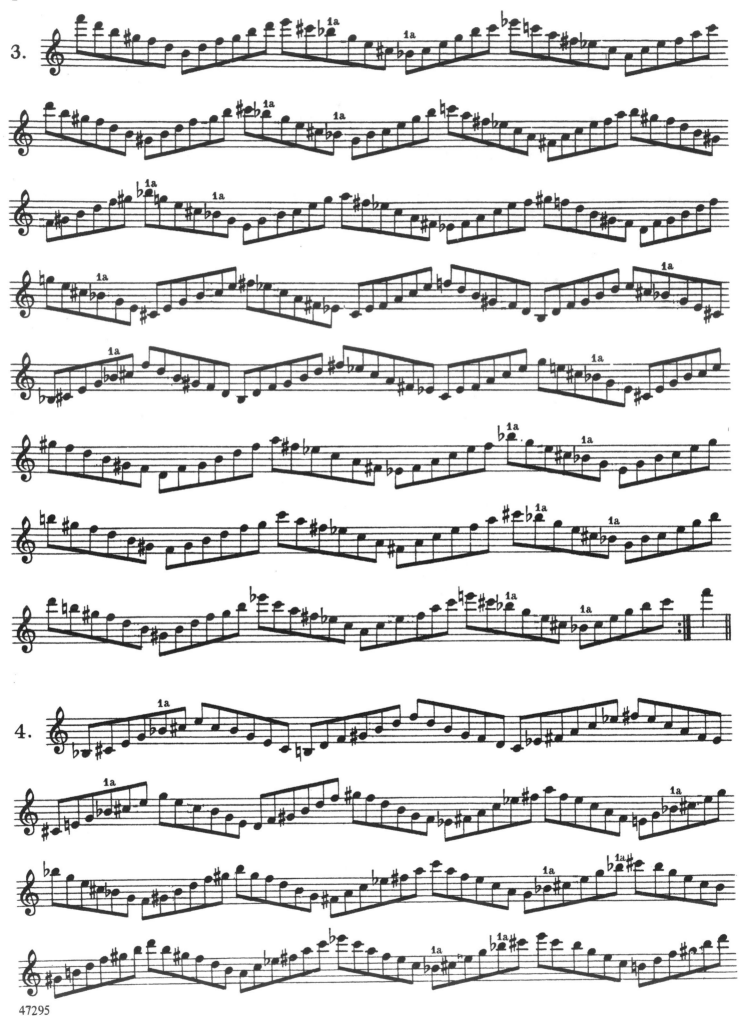

6

8.

9.

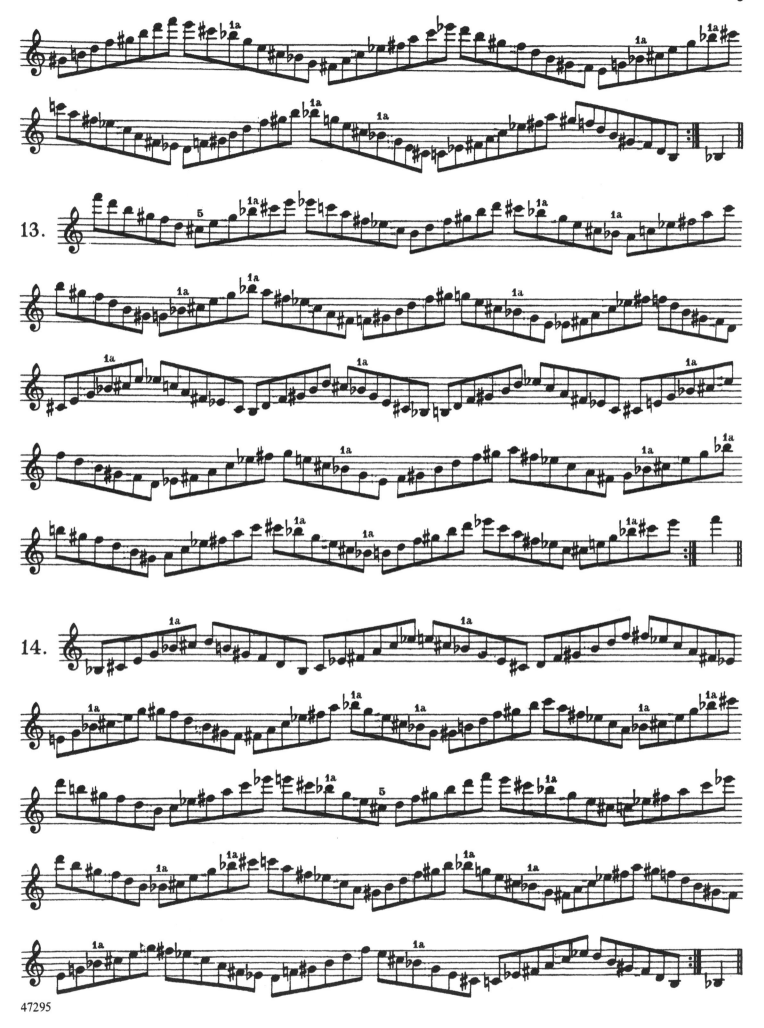

10

12

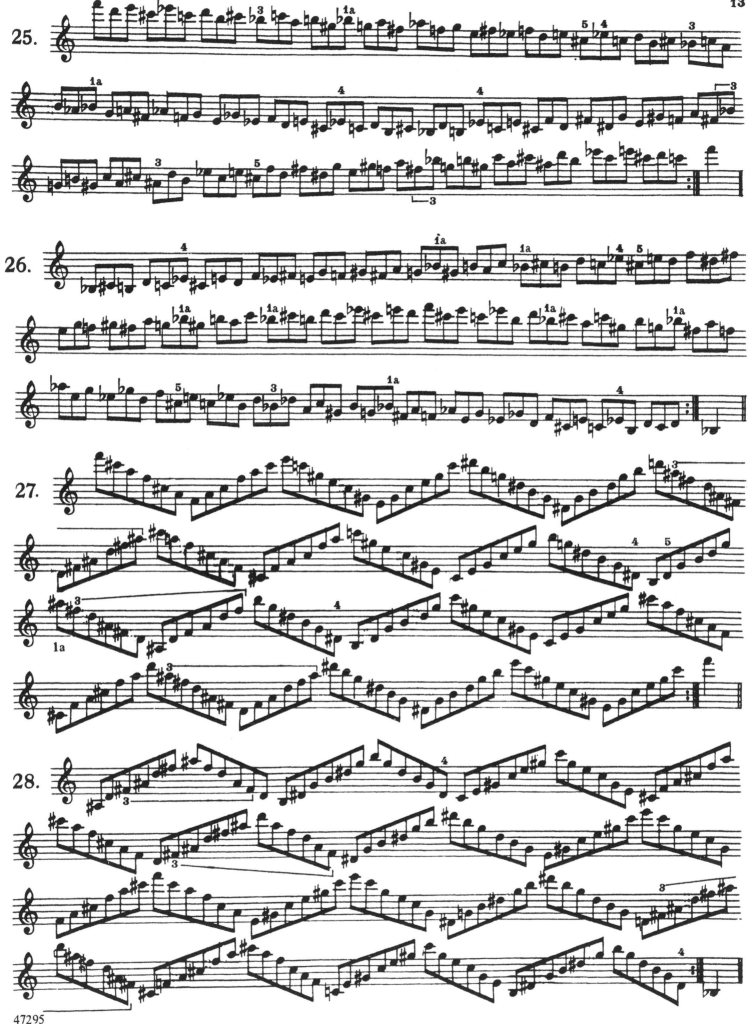

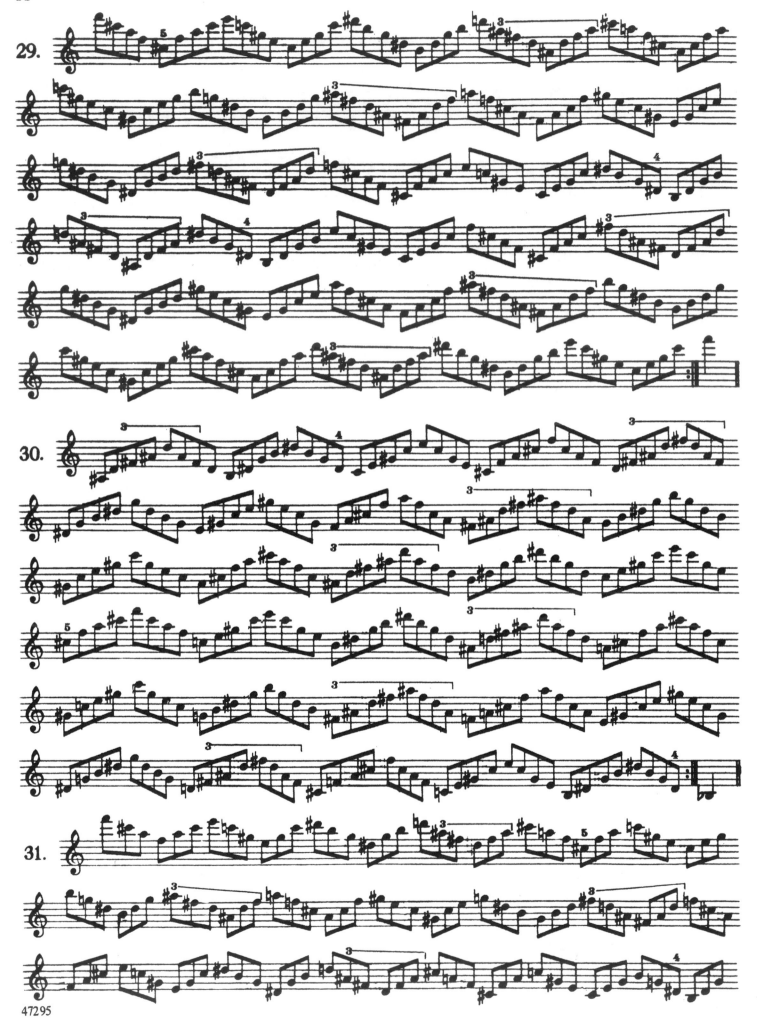

34

35.

36.

37.

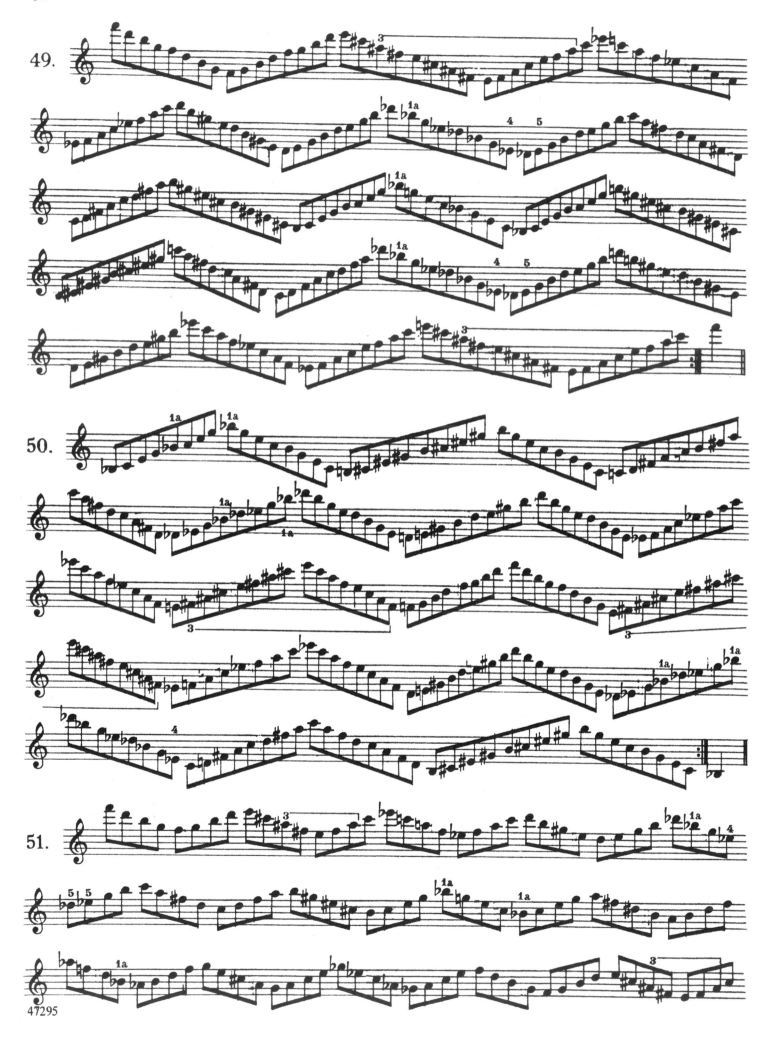

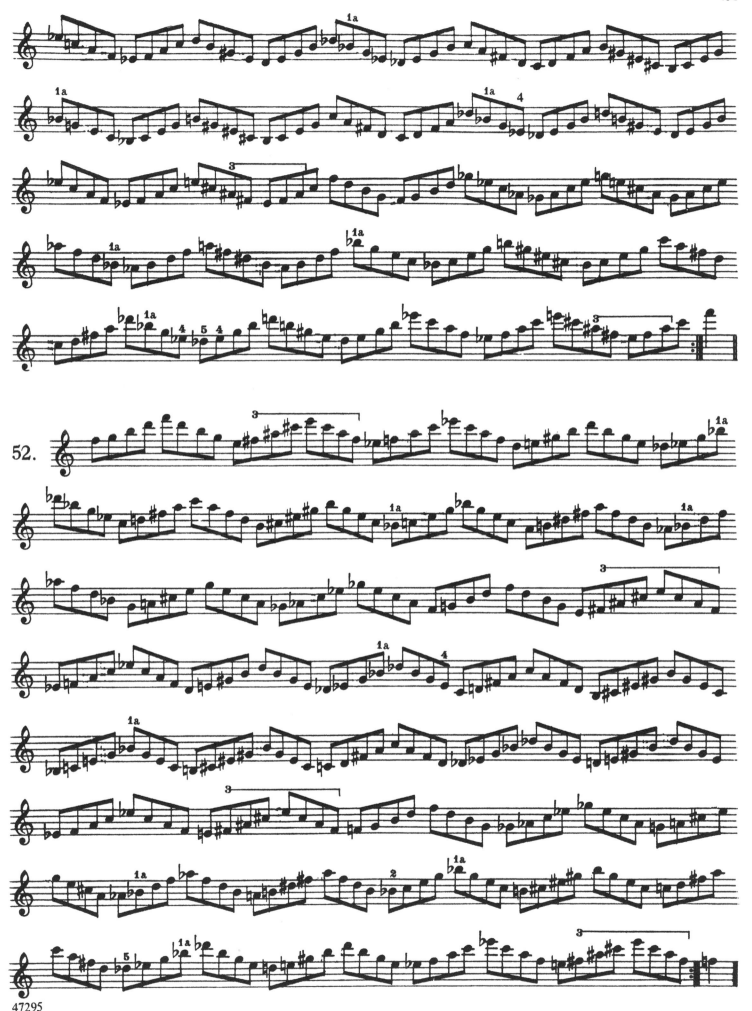

52.

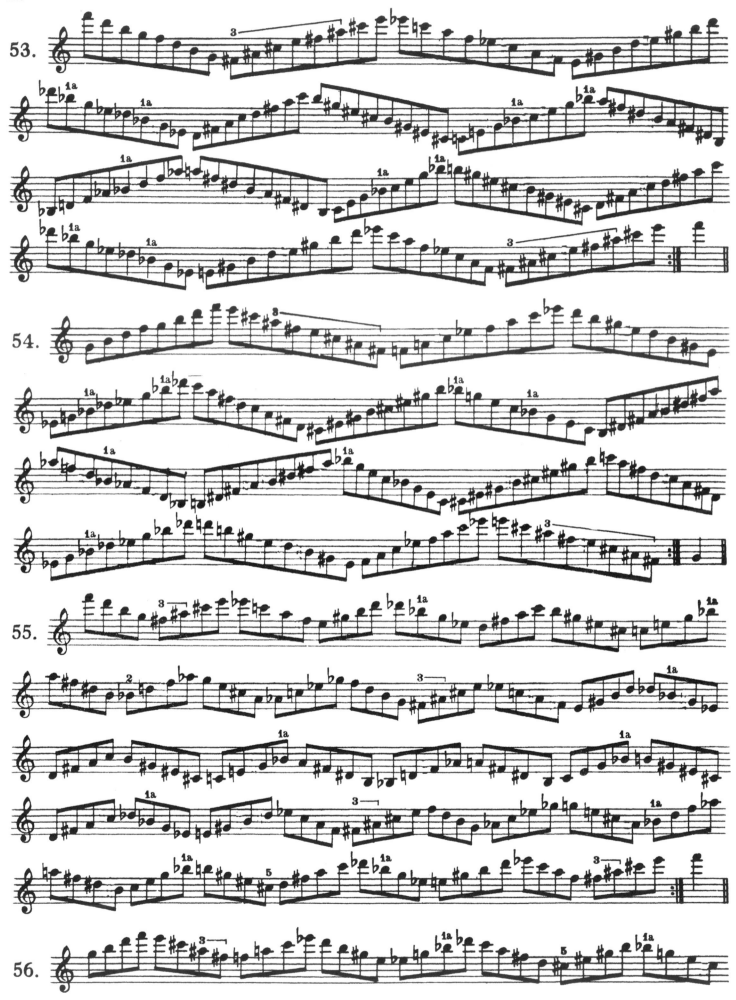

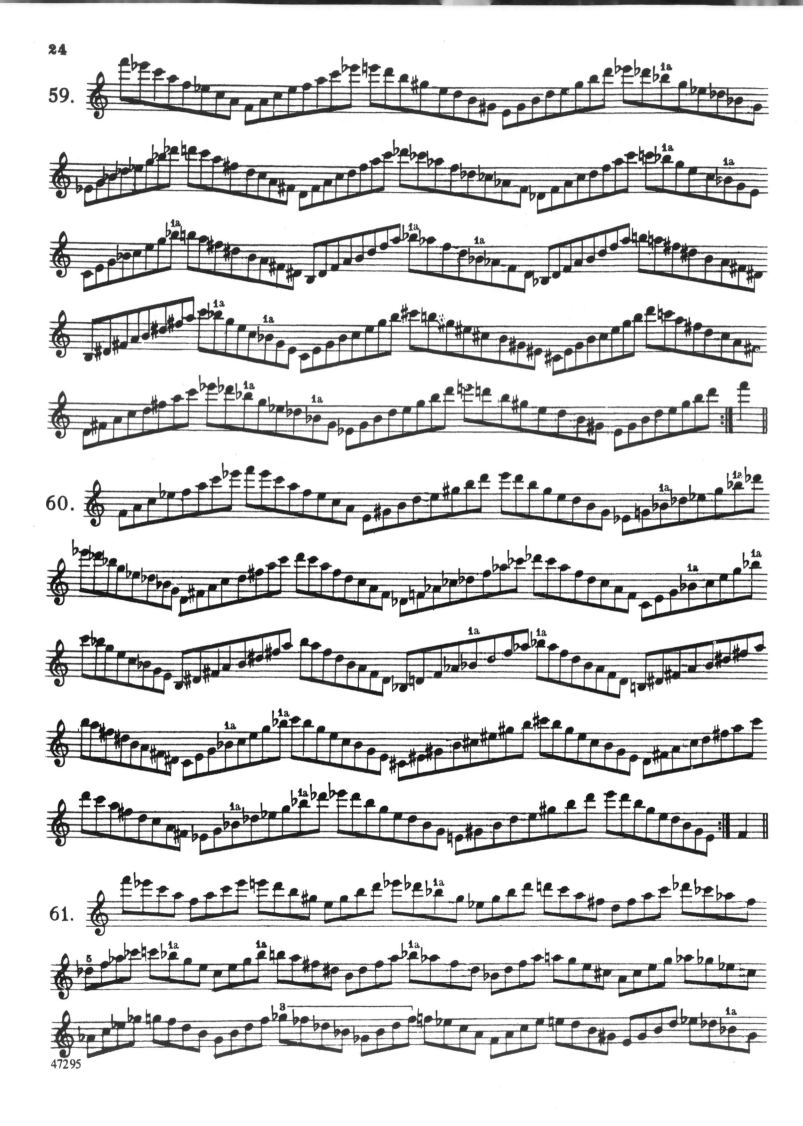

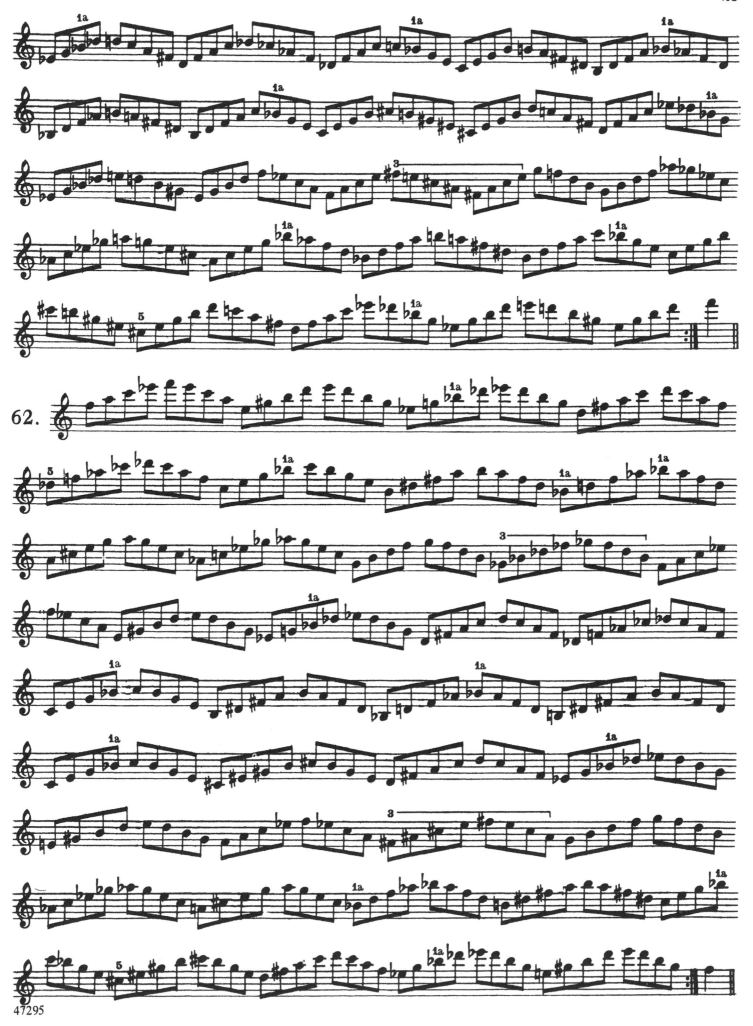

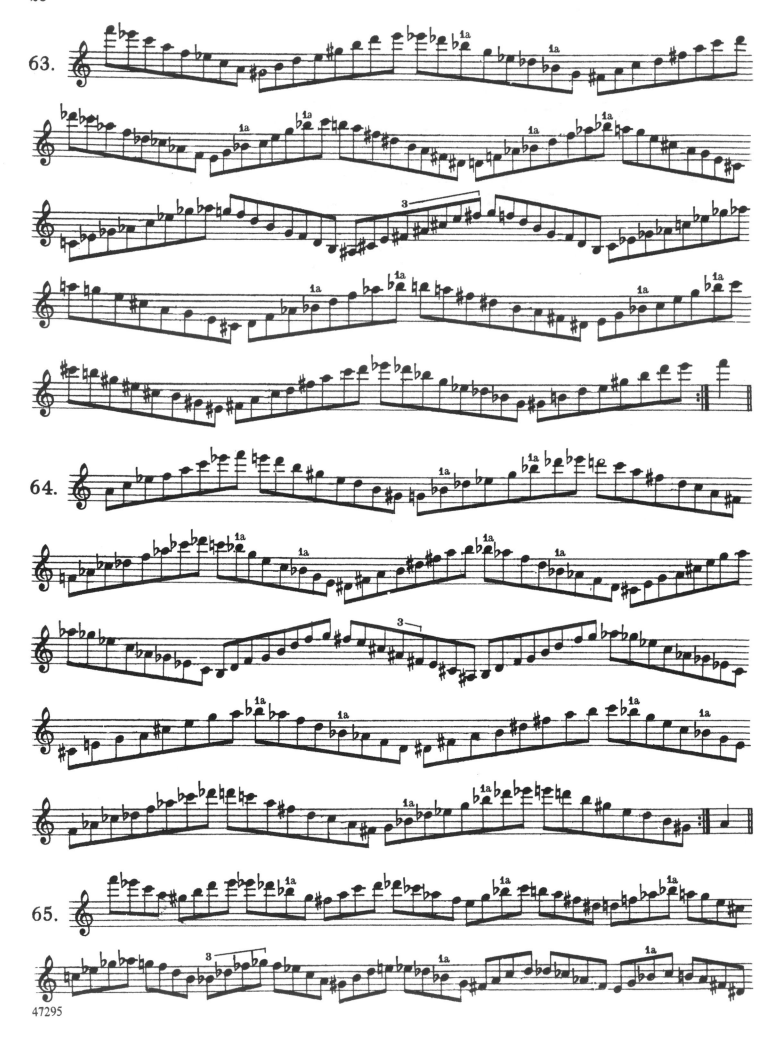

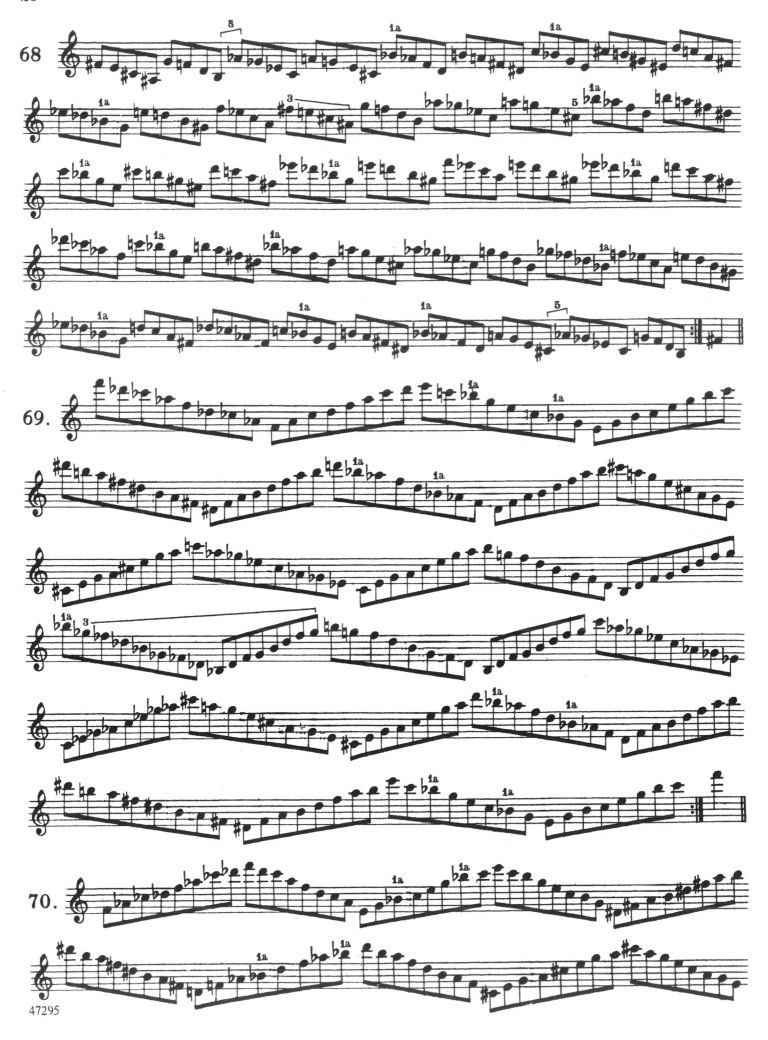

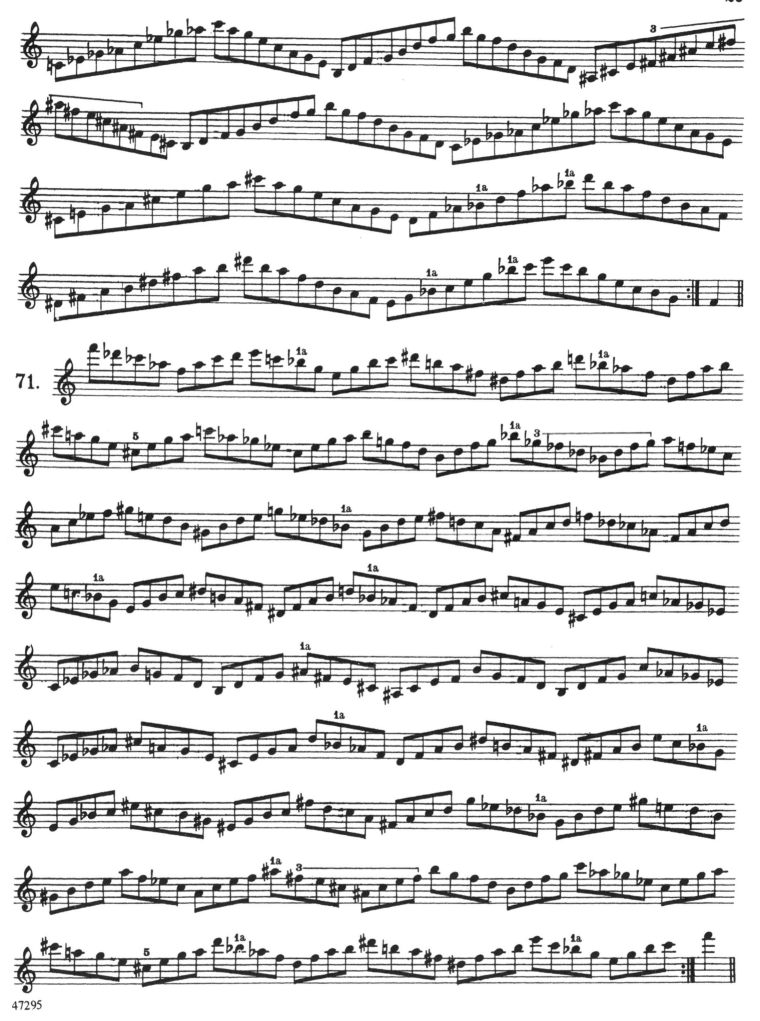

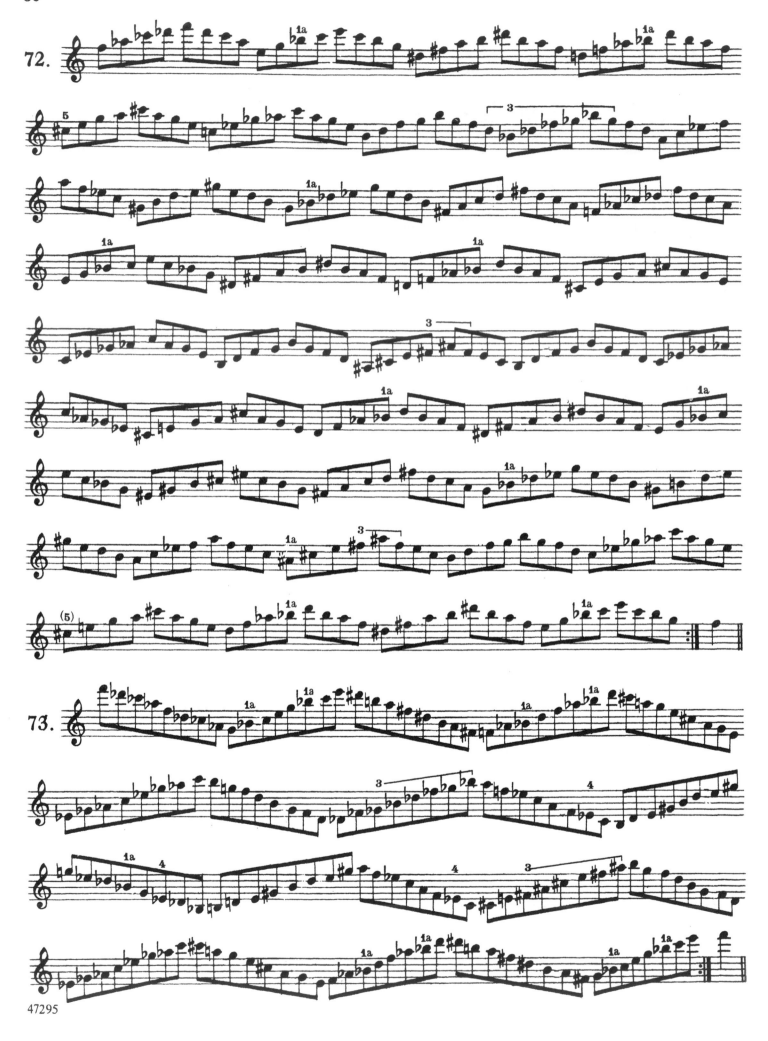

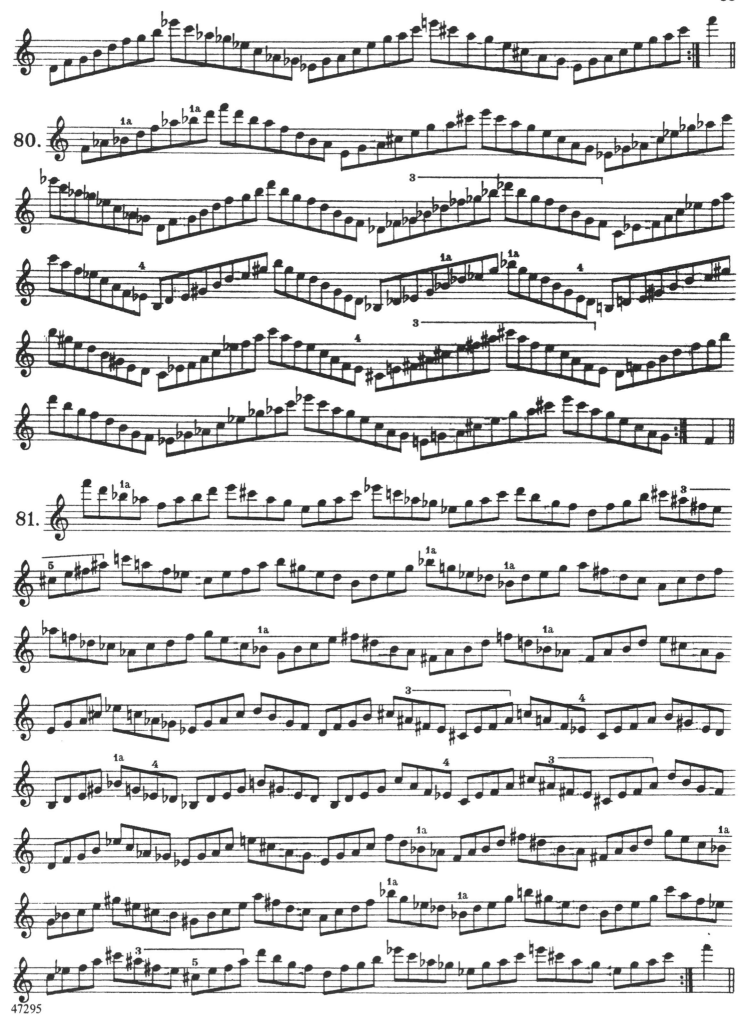

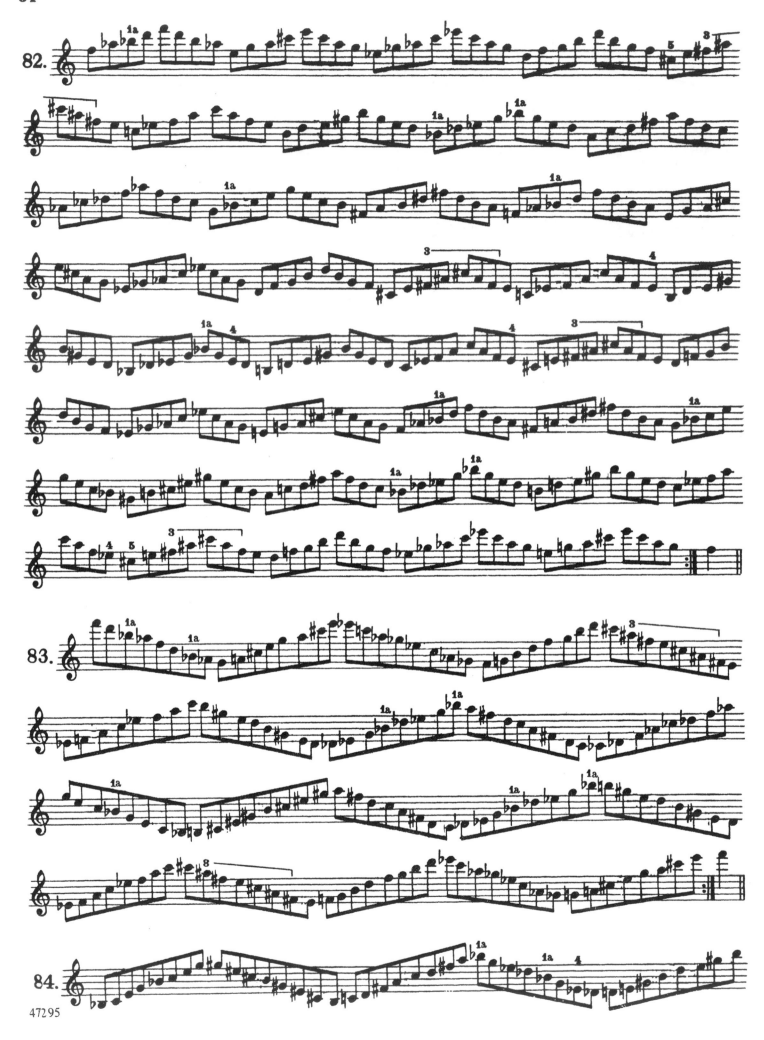

36

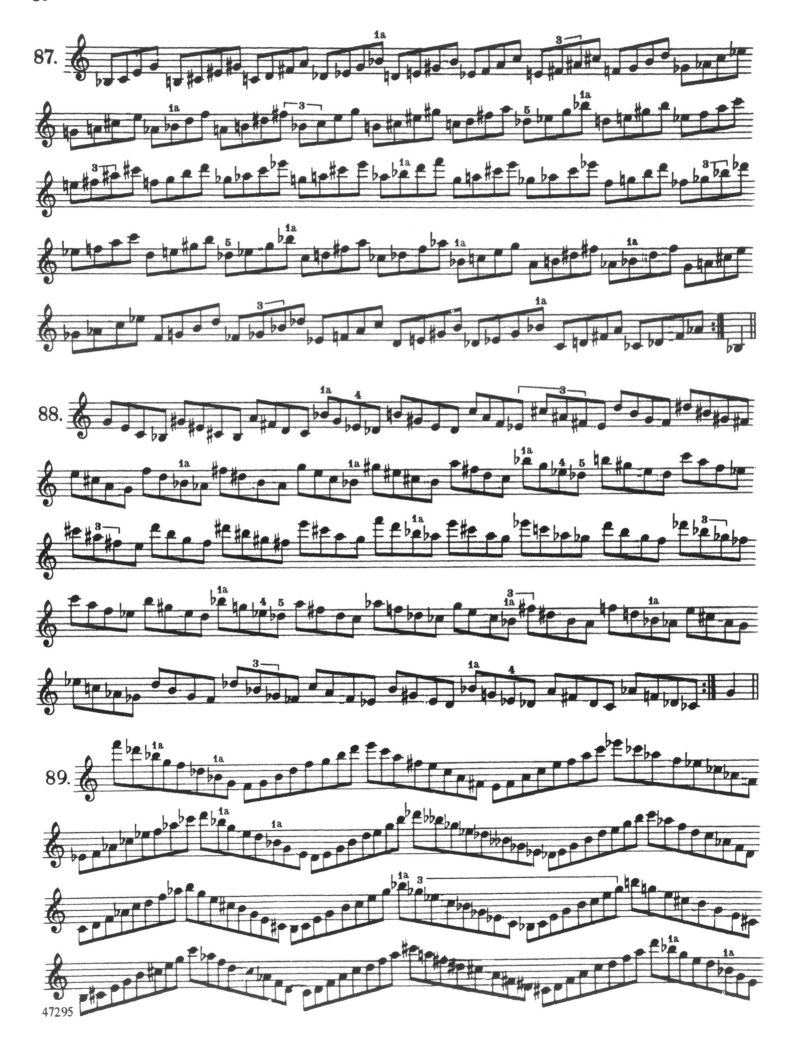

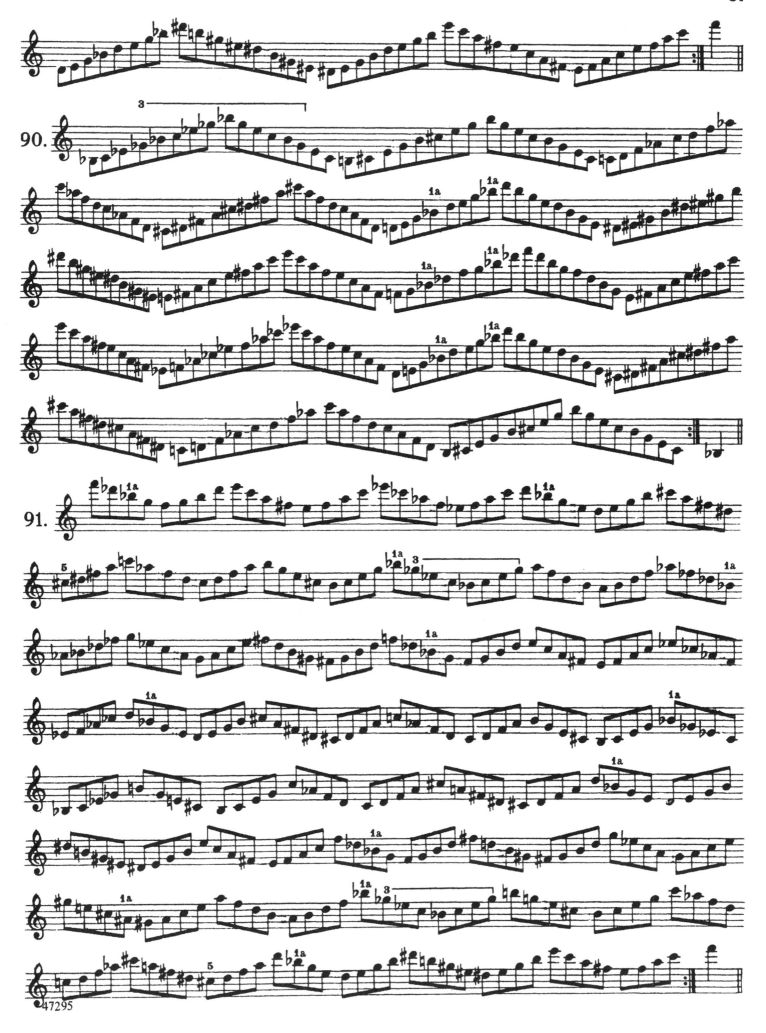

90.

91.

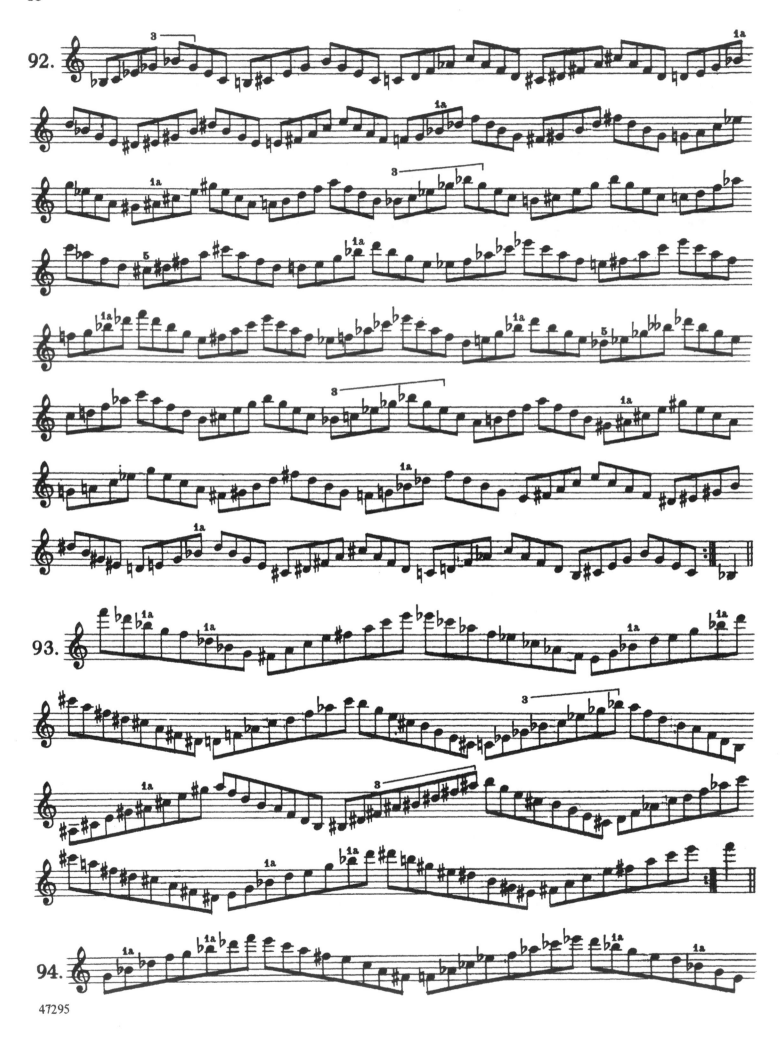

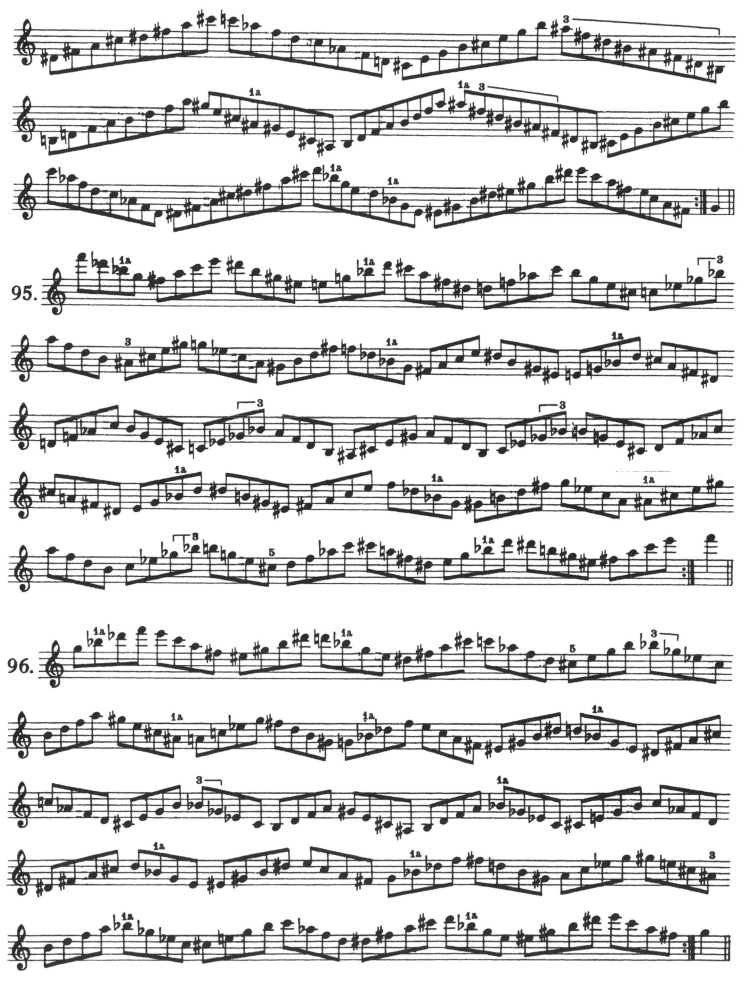

95.

96.

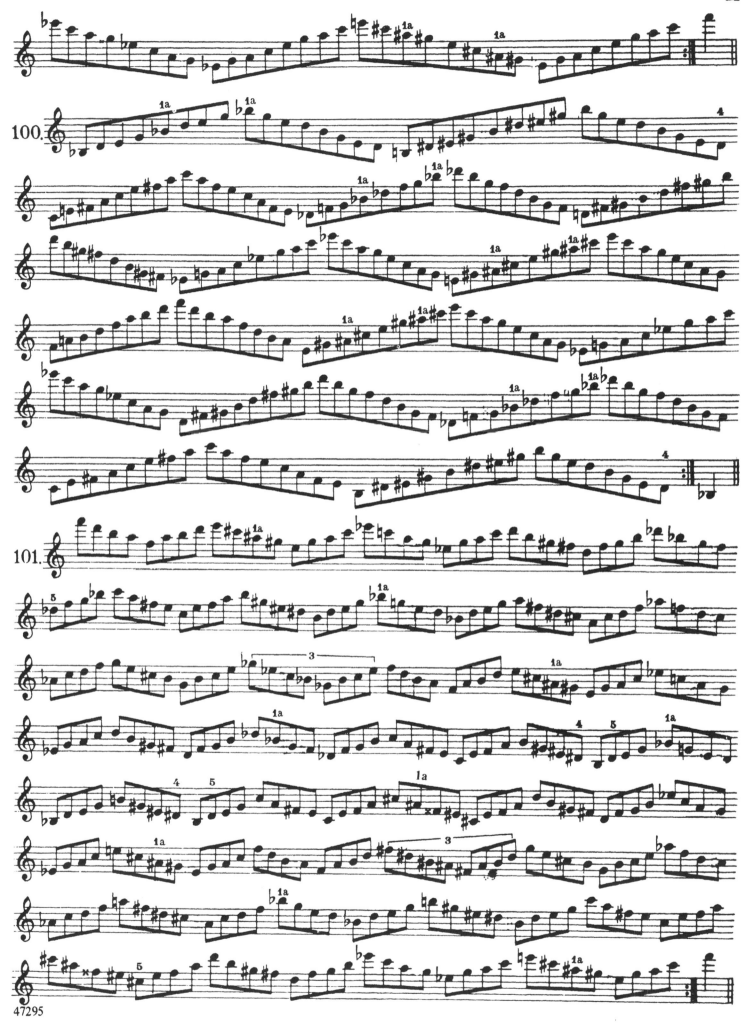

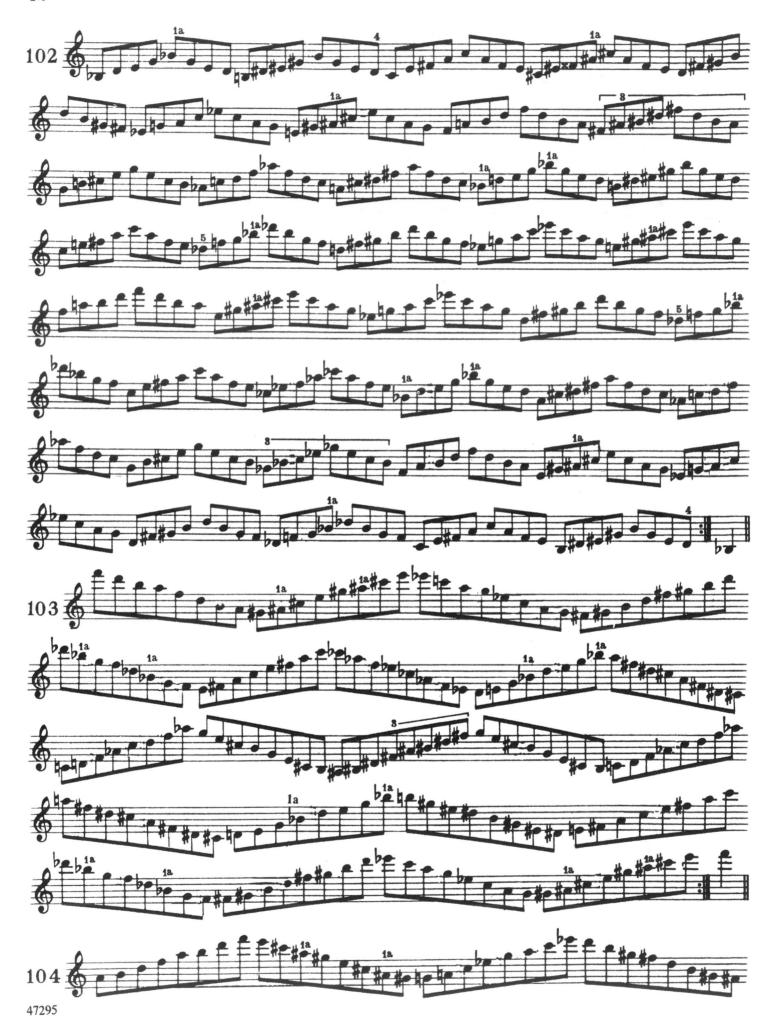

44

47295

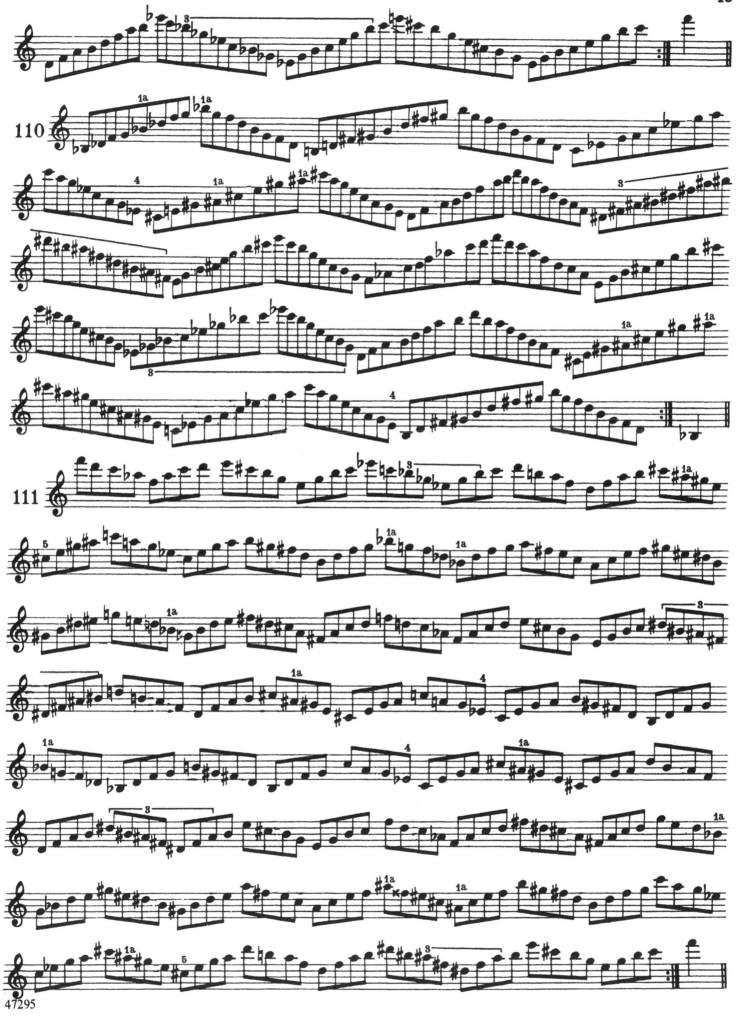

46

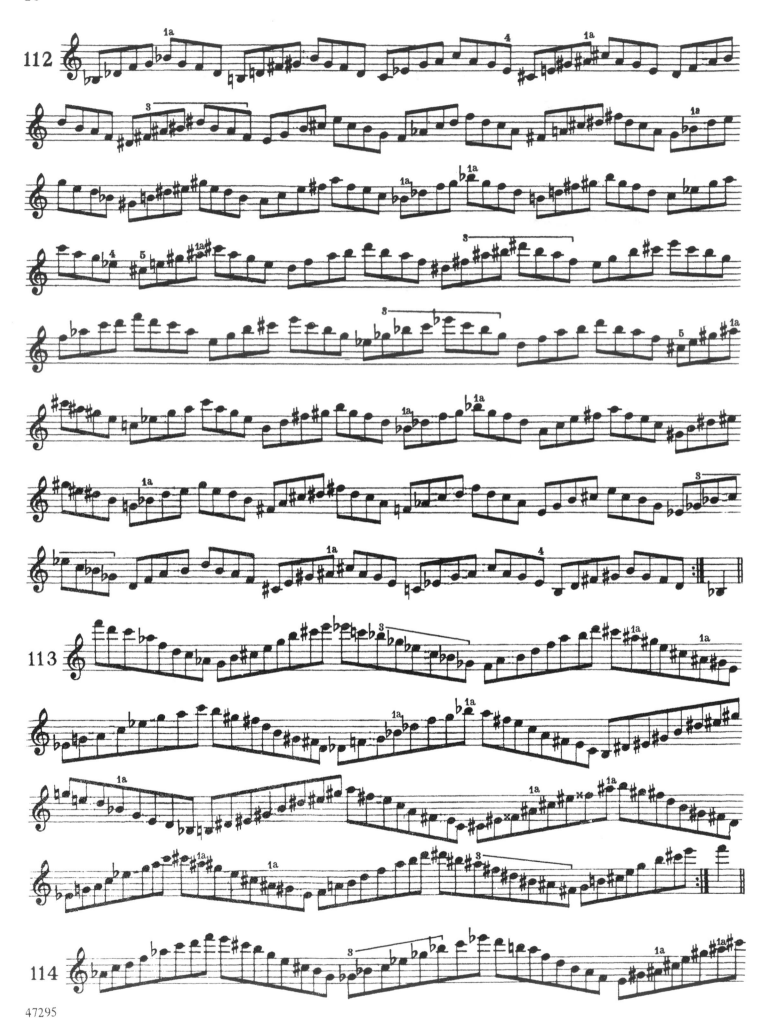

47295

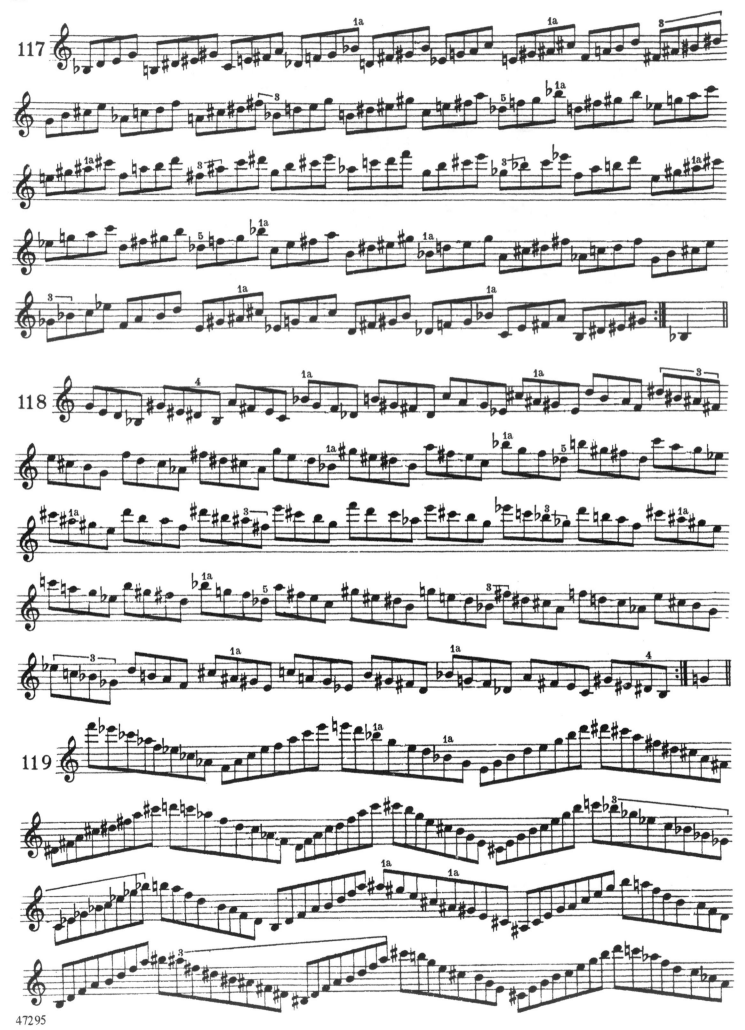

49

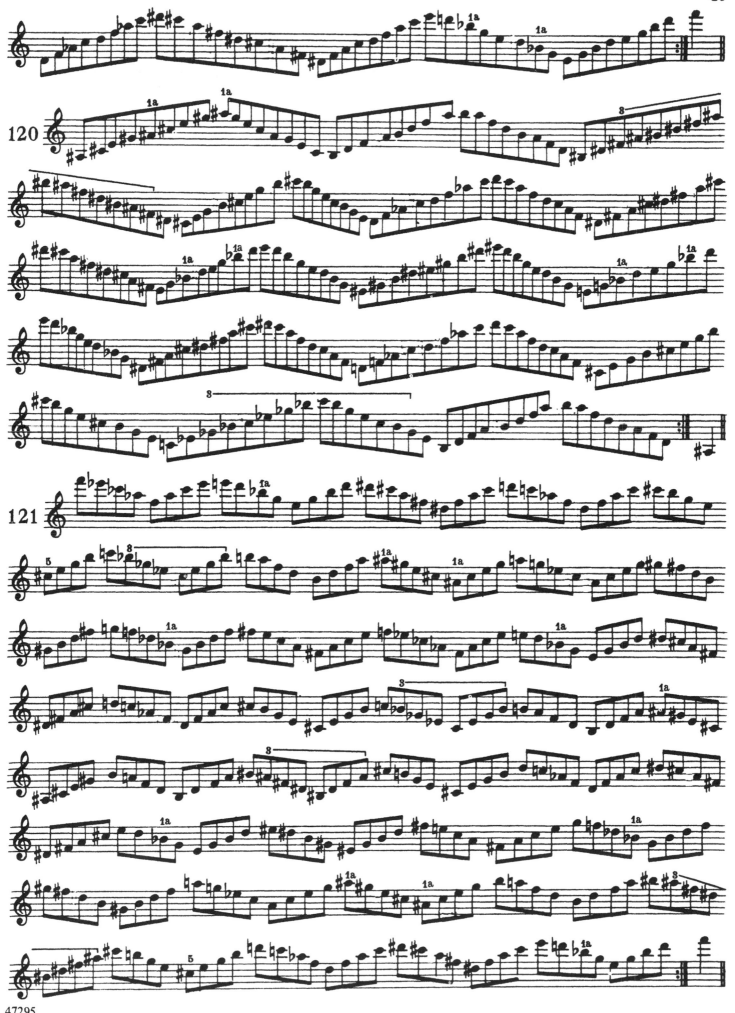

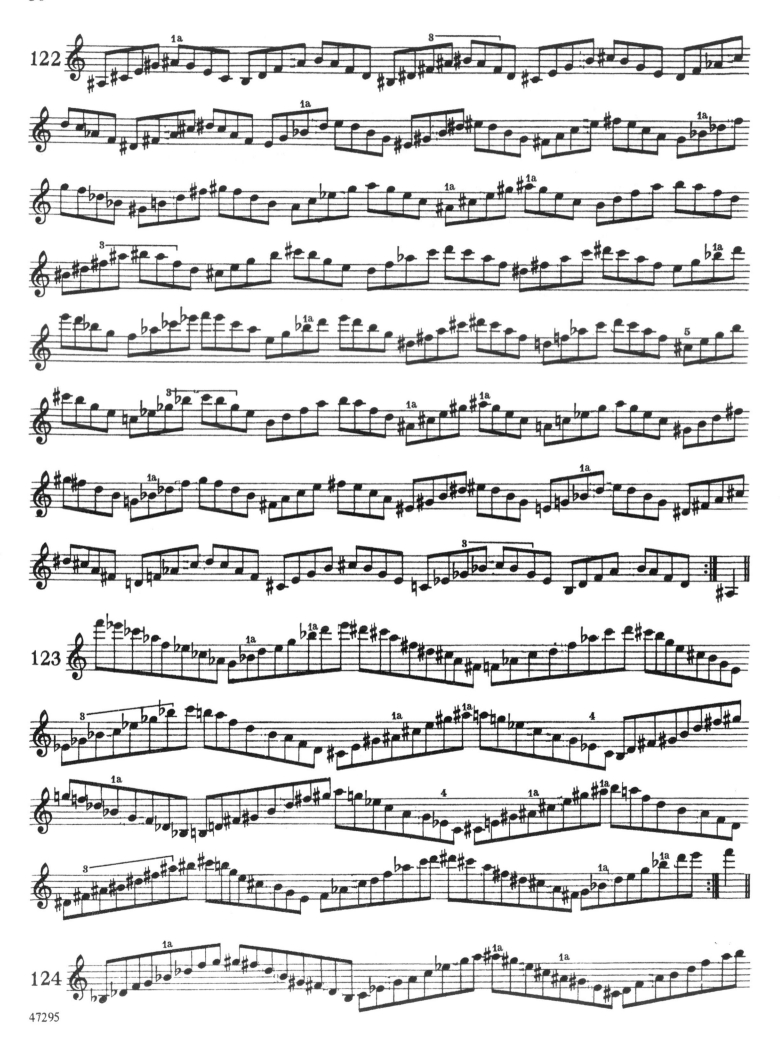

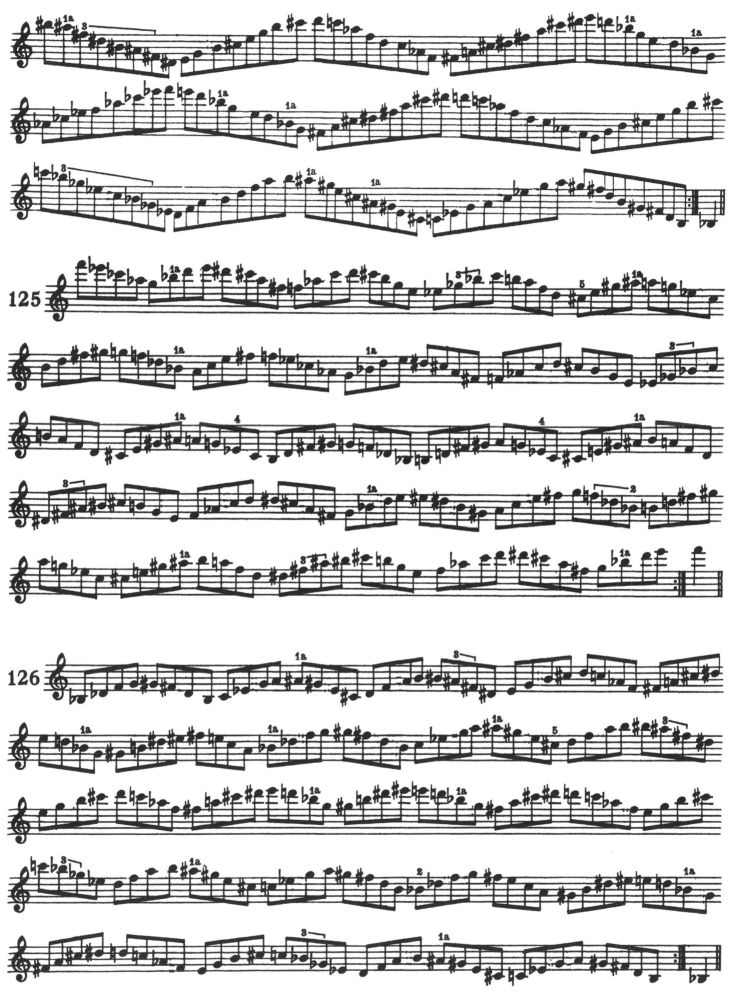

125

126